GET MY NEW BOOK!

As an exclusive and special gift for readers of *The Magic of Short Books,* I have authored a must-have book, which is the perfect complement to this book because it goes into detail on ways to make money with a *free book* offer!

The Magic of Free Books is an advanced book that I wrote to show business owners 51 specific and proven tactics to turn a *free book* into new customers. There is **NO OTHER BOOK** like it and you can **ONLY GET IT HERE...**

SPECIAL READER BONUS

www.MarketingWithFreeBooks.com

ALSO BY MIKE CAPUZZI

Dream, Inc.

The Ultimate Success Secret (with Dan Kennedy)

3 Steps to Incredible Response

The Entrepreneur's Guide to Marketing with PURLs

High Impact Marketing Manifesto

Masters of the Mastermind

Just Do This

Main Street Author

WIN WIN WIN

The Magic of Gratitude

7 Habits of Super Successful Mattress Retailers

The 100-Page Book (an Amazon #1 Best Seller)

The Magic of Free Books

*Discover My Simple, Step-by Step Formula
for Creating an Effective Customer Attraction Book*

THE MAGIC OF
SHORT BOOKS

FAST **EASY** **SMART** **HELPFUL**

MIKE CAPUZZI

PUBLISHED BY BITE SIZED BOOKS
A DIVISION OF PERSISTENT MARKETING, INC.

Print ISBN: 978-1-7325127-5-7
eBook ISBN: 978-1-7341187-0-4

121120

BITE SIZED
BOOKS

Bite Sized Books publishes short, helpful books or shooks™ for Main Street business owners to attract new customers. Shooks are easy-to-create, quick-to-read short books. They are designed to be read by prospective customers, clients or patients, in about an hour. Bite Sized Books offers a painless process to enable entrepreneurs and business owners to benefit from the authority that comes from being a published author, without the hassle and time commitment normally associated with writing a book. Do you have an idea for a bite sized book you would like us to publish? Visit BiteSizedBooks.com for more details.

CONTENTS

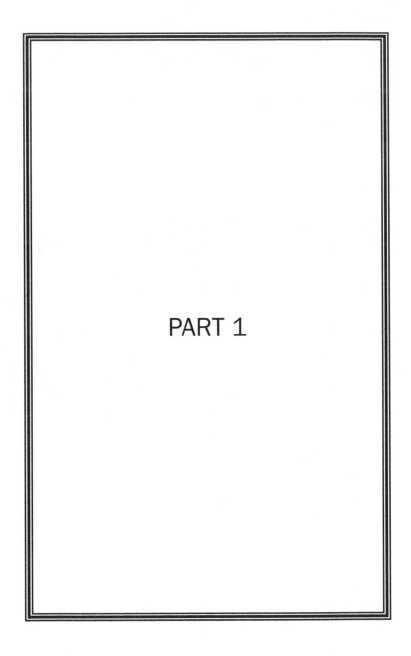

PART 1

WELCOME

FOREWORD

How do you pick out a wizard from the crowd (assuming he's in plain clothes and not wearing his pointed hat or brandishing his wand)? You won't, unless you catch sight of him doing some magic.

This short book gives you a rare opportunity to catch a wizard at work.

I've been running our BiteFX software business (computer animations for dentists) for well over a decade and realized early on that my product creation talents that got us started weren't enough to guarantee our long-term success. We needed to market BiteFX constantly and better than my instincts or knowledge could do. So, I've been devouring all sorts of materials on "how to market your business well" for several years. I first heard of Mike Capuzzi because of his excellent CopyDoodles® product and signed up for his High Impact Marketing emails.

Whereas most other marketing guru emails felt overpowering with the gurus' charisma, Mike's communications were always practical and down-to-earth. You felt you were hearing from a real, straightforward guy who had simple, but great, tips to share even though he was a "big name" lauded by numerous other marketing gurus. (Confirmed when I recently attended a conference organized by Bill Glazer featuring famous speaker after famous speaker, but whose name was mentioned most often by those speakers?—"Mike Capuzzi.")

My perception of Mike as the "real, straightforward guy" has been confirmed as I've worked more closely with him over the last year or so. First, I appreciated his willingness to talk to me as I was exploring some of his mentoring services, and then the egoless help and advice he has provided in both group and one-on-one settings has been priceless.

He makes you feel comfortable while inspiring you with great suggestions founded on his years of guiding small business owners. That's why I suggest to you that Mike is a wizard and that he is sharing some magic with you in this aptly titled short book, *The Magic of Short Books.*

Perhaps you're like me and have never thought of writing a book until now, or perhaps you've always wanted to write a book but considered it to be out of your reach or never achievable because of one stumbling block or another. In either case I'd say that you've found the right book and the right person to help you overcome the obstacles to make your book a reality. That's certainly been my experience.

It's only a few months ago that I became convinced that a short book would be an excellent marketing tool for our BiteFX business. I am so grateful I engaged Mike as my mentor and coach. You'll see in these pages that he has considerable experience in writing and using short books—experience he shares willingly and positively—I always feel encouraged after talking with Mike.

Without his help, our shook, *Becoming Your Patients' Hero*, wouldn't exist today. There could have been so many bumps in the road that would have delayed or derailed us, but Mike magically smoothed them away, and we proceeded rapidly to completion. So, soak in all the lessons he shares!

Are short books really magical? It appears that way! I've now shared our book at two dental conferences. At one, I'd say 10% to 15% of the attendees might have looked at our BiteFX software product if I was lucky, but over 70% bought our book.

At the other, I had just two minutes to present to the audience after the last official break at which attendees could visit exhibitors (of which I was one)—

kind of a no-hope situation—yet 25 of those attendees rushed out at a fortuitous unofficial break to get the book. Plus, a CEO of a major teaching organization who I'd been having difficulty getting time with, accepted a copy of our book and later told me she'd enjoyed reading it on her return flight home. These are all door-opening connections that we wouldn't have had, had we not had a short book to offer.

Mike may not present himself as a wizard, but by the end of reading *The Magic of Short Books*, you're going to have a sense of the magic he yields, and you definitely want to take up his offer of a shook assessment and call. There aren't many wizards who are available in this way, and I'd recommend doing it quickly as it won't be long before Mike's schedule is filled to the brim (of his hat)!

Doug Brown, BiteFX CEO
Co-author of *Becoming Your Patients' Hero*

WHO SHOULD READ THIS BOOK?

E ven though this is a short book, designed to be read in about an hour, I don't want to waste your time if it's not a good fit. Please take a few minutes and read this entire section to see if *The Magic of Short Books* is a smart investment of your time. I wrote this short book for three reasons:

1. To shift your focus from traditional, *everybody has one* marketing tools like business cards and brochures, to an authority-building, customer-attraction system centered around your own short book.

2. To share a unique type of **short, helpful book** (shook™) I believe most, if not all, business owners should leverage in their business, and give you a step-by-step formula for creating one.

3. To invite readers to connect with me so we can determine if working together to publish their shook is the right next step.

I am a *"what you see is what you get"* kind of guy, and I'm not shying away from the fact that while my intention is to open your eyes to a new marketing asset for your business, I also want readers who get what I have to offer, to reach out to me to see if working together makes sense.

I am perplexed when people criticize business book authors for "selling too much" in their books because, in my opinion, not enough business-related books offer readers a "next step." This next step should be a helpful continuation of the book's promise, and I believe is a critical part of the book.

Today, more than ever before, people are seeking quality information to help them make smart decisions, save time and avoid mistakes. If you and your products/services can do this, why would you be squeamish about letting people know how you can help them and offering a logical next step?

I am unapologetically "selling" in this shook, not only the concept of a shook and why I think it's a superior type of book for you to create but also why working directly with me to publish your short, helpful book is a smart and effective shortcut to success and quick completion.

If you're good with all this so far, allow me to further drill down into what type of business owner I've written this shook for and who I think can benefit from publishing a shook or series of shooks.

I believe just about any business owner can benefit and profit from having a shook working for them in their business, but there are four "types" of business owners who make <u>ideal</u> shook authors.

1. Healthcare professionals, including dentists, physicians, chiropractors, therapists

2. Professional service providers, including, lawyers, insurance agents, consultants

3. High-ticket or luxury product/service providers, including, certain types of retailers, real estate professionals

4. Complicated product/service providers, including, software developers, manufacturers

These business owners have unique needs to explain, clarify and position their products and/or services, which I believe can be best served with a shook and a shook-centric marketing system.

Finally, *The Magic of Short Books* was written for the person who agrees with these seven beliefs:

1. Time is the most precious gift in our lives, and if we can connect and help others while taking up less, we will be rewarded.

2. The written word containing useful information is one of the best ways to communicate why your products or services will help others solve a problem or take advantage of a new opportunity.

3. Sharing your personal story and stories of how you have helped others will uniquely humanize you and be the beginning of a mutually beneficial relationship between you and your readers.

4. You only have a moment to grab the interest of your targeted prospective customers amid the on-slaught of competing marketing messages they are exposed to every day. Once you have their attention with a shook in their hands, you will have a more focused opportunity to communicate why they should invest in your product or service.

5. A real, professionally "constructed" printed book is one of the most powerful advantages and unique game changers in the business world for positioning you and attracting more ideal customers.

6. Short books are a welcomed relief from *books with bloat*, which contain unnecessary filler and are started but typically never completed by readers.

7. A shook is a worthy business asset for you to create, and working with me is the key to getting it done fast and pain-free.

If you are like me and believe you can balance helpful written content with making the case for you and your business, and you are not afraid of making specific, "next step" offers for your readers to take, I wrote this shook for you, so please keep reading.

MY PROMISE TO YOU

I promise to make *The Magic of Short Books* a valuable use of your money, time and attention. Within the next 60 minutes or so, my intention is to open your eyes to the possibility and value of publishing your own customer-attraction short book and motivate you to take action and get started with your own short book.

I will minimize the hype and bloat (found in a lot of business books), get right to the point and share the essentials of what you need to know to author a customer-attraction short book.

Before we move on, I have two reminders for you. Regardless of whether you call the consumers you serve, patients, students, or clients—for simplicity I will refer to them as "customers" throughout the rest of this shook.

Also, I am not going to spend much time trying to convince you to write a book for your business. There are a number of books that make the case for why you should have a book, and I am 100% convinced most business owners should have a short, helpful book working for them 24/7. If you need more information or inspiration, a simple search on Amazon will reveal many options.

I'm assuming if you are reading these words, you know the power of what having a professionally designed, printed book can do for you and your business. Being a business owner who is also an author allows you to advertise, market and sell at a higher, more sophisticated level where you attract customers instead of pursuing them.

This is the magic of short books!

INTRODUCTION

Since you're reading these words, I'm assuming you're OK with what I've shared so far and you are ready to join me for a rewarding 60 minutes as I share the magic of short books.

It's important for you to know I love books and have done so from a very young age. My maternal grandmother was a voracious reader and got me hooked on books early. I've tried hard to share this love of books with my two daughters. In 2018, my oldest daughter Caroline, who was a senior in high school, published her first book, *Dog Joy*, which featured dog rescue stories. The neat thing about her book is that it generated thousands of dollars for dog rescues even before the first copy was printed.

I have a large library of books, including several rare first editions. I have published seven books prior to this one and have helped several business owners publish their own books. To me, there is nothing like a real, <u>printed</u> book, and there is nothing like the feeling of handing somebody your book and watching their expression as they realize you're the author.

But as I stated previously, I am not a book "purist" and don't subscribe to the common way of thinking books should be void of promotion, marketing and selling. I also don't believe books should be filled with unnecessary content simply to reach a specific page count so the publisher can charge a certain amount for the book.

This is why I've developed the shook—a short, helpful book, which follows a specific three-part Capuzzi-developed formula:

1. Shooks are designed so you can create them quickly and easily. Since they contain about 25–50% of the words a typical business book does, you don't have to spend months/years writing them, and most of my clients complete their shooks in 8-12 weeks, from initial idea to finished printed copies.

2. Shooks are designed so your targeted reader can read them, cover to cover in a single sitting, in about an hour or so. I personally don't subscribe to the notion, *"It doesn't matter if a person reads your book, you just want to have one."* I believe if you have something important to share, that will help your readers, why wouldn't you want them to read your entire book?

3. Shooks are *direct response books* and have embedded *Passive* Calls-to-Action that give your readers additional value while enabling you to build a valuable database of prospects. Shooks also present your readers with a clear, *active* "next step" so they know exactly what to do next.

While some may scoff at the concept of a shook, it's been my experience regular people **LOVE** them. They don't take much time to read. They help solve a single problem or present a single opportunity, and they offer a chance for readers to continue the relationship with the author.

My goal with *The Magic of Short Books* is to open your eyes to the profitable possibilities of what a shook can do for you and your business. If you've never written a book before, a shook is the perfect type of book for you to start with (no novice mountain climber climbs Mt. Everest first), and if you are an experienced author, a shook or series of shooks could be a perfect addition to your existing library of books.

The shook you are reading at this moment, *The Magic of Short Books*, is the first in my Shook Success Series. There are three other shooks in this series. Learn more about them on page 117.

Finally, I want you to keep this in mind as you read on—**you can author a short, helpful book for the benefit of your ideal reader!**

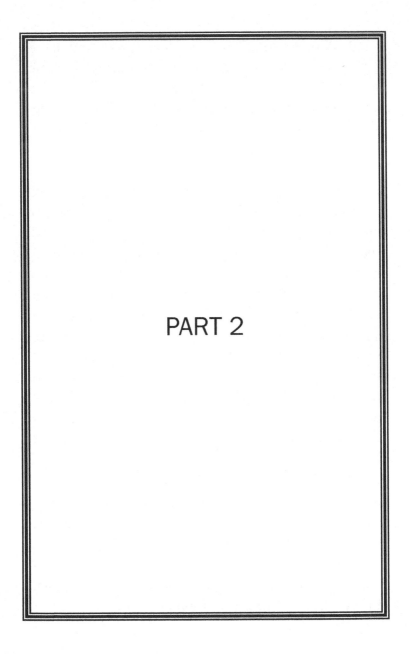

PART 2

HOW TO BE PITHY
AND POWERFUL

SHOOK IN ACTION

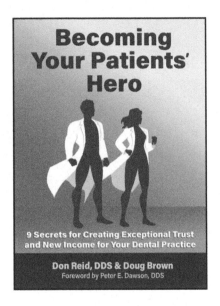

Title:	*Becoming Your Patients' Hero*
Authors:	Don Reid and Doug Brown
Shook hook:	Nine secrets for creating exceptional trust and new income from your dental practice
Page count:	132
Active CTA:	Software system test-drive
Passive CTA:	Bonus tools to help implement the strategies shared in the shook

CHAPTER 1

THE WORLD NEEDS MORE SHORT, HELPFUL BOOKS

B ooks have been an effective way for business owners to offer helpful information to solve a specific problem for over 100 years. In my research, I have found advertisements that have featured a "free book" as far back as 1903, when the Ostermoor Mattress Company offered their book, *The Test of Time*, to individuals interested in getting a better night's sleep.

Throughout the 20th century, books were offered to consumers, who have a specific problem or desire, as a tool to help them. It's no different in the 21st century, and after a review of printed ads, television commercials and social media marketing, you still find books being used as a way to help and connect.

A book, focused on a single topic with a single call -to-action, is still one of the most effective "attract new customer" assets you can create. As I mentioned earlier, there are many books already written about the importance of having a book working for you and your business.

But there is one critical difference today than in previous years—the lack of free time available for people to read your book and for you to write it.

Most consumers (my guess is 95%) don't have the time or attention span to read long books, regardless of the subject's importance or interest level. They may start with the best of intentions, but after a few chapters, something else gets their attention and the book is put down, never to be completed.

Unfortunately, the promise of the book, the reason they started to read it, is never fulfilled, which is why there is a trend for traditional business books to be getting shorter—not quite shook length, but down to less than 300 pages. How many people have time to read a 300-page book these days?

Just recently, I was given a business book as a gift—it's by a famous Internet marketing expert. As soon as I opened the box and saw it, my first reaction was, "That's a really long book." Coming in at over 400 pages, the book's length resulted in the immediate (and typical) decision to simply lay it aside and maybe get to it at some point in the future.

Contrast this to your perception when you received this shook you are reading now. Did its size intimidate you or invite you to read it? Did you find my promise of a short, quick read appealing?

Think about your own reading habits. When was the last time you actually finished a book (other than the anticipated finishing of this one)? If you're like the business owners I surveyed for this shook, more than 80% of you have not finished a business book you've started within the past year. I get it and I am in the same boat for a number of reasons.

Yes, there are times you have picked up a book thinking one thing and then after starting it you realize it's a different thing, but that's not the critical mistake many authors make. I think people make their books unnecessarily long for the wrong reasons, with the main one being they simply don't know how to create content that is pithy and powerful.

French author Blaise Pascal wrote in 1657, "I have made this letter longer than usual, only because I have not had the time to make it shorter."

Re-read that quote again, because it's powerful and an important reminder for crafting content.

Developing a short, concise and powerful message is no easy task, and it takes more effort to create it than to bloviate and spew everything you know about your product or service. I call it going from "blah, blah, blah to BIG AH-HA" and if you can master this important writing skill, you will profit.

Shooks are laser-focused on a single big message, and the good news is a shook and working with me solves both of these problems. It gives your targeted reader a single-focus book, which can be read quickly and easily thereby giving them the sense of accomplishment we all get when we finish a task we started (this is an "invisible" but important benefit of a shook).

It gives you a simple formula to craft content that is focused, powerful and in less time than required by traditional-length books. Shooks are a win-win for your reader and you!

Even though we are not focused on becoming a New York Times bestseller, there have been short books on the list over the years, most notably *Who Moved My Cheese?* and *The One Minute Manager.* The former has 96 pages and sold 28 million copies from 1998-2017, and the latter has 111 pages and sold 13 million copies in 10 years. The list of classic fictional short books is a long one, with *A Christmas Carol* and *Of Mice and Men* on it.

Never underestimate the power of short books, and in many situations, less can mean more.

If today's consumer wants information in shorter, more digestible "chunks," why not give it to them in a way that makes it easier for them to consume? Trying to fight this growing trend is futile and learning how to adapt to make it work for you is critical.

Don't forget that being able to add the title of "author" to your credentials increases your perceived worth, which means you can charge more for your products and services and minimize resistance to price-shopping.

By crafting your business book as a shook, you make it more likely to be read in its entirety, giving you a better chance readers will complete your call-to-action and eventually become a customer.

As I like to say, "Don't write a book, publish a shook!"

SHOOK IN ACTION

Title:	*I Thought This Thing Was Safe!*
Authors:	Daniel J. O'Brien and Alison J. Russell
Shook hook:	Know exactly what to do if you are injured by a faulty consumer product
Page count:	100
Active CTA:	Call office for an initial consultation with the authors
Passive CTA:	Call office for an initial consultation with the authors

CHAPTER 2

SHOOKS ARE DIRECT RESPONSE BOOKS

Shooks are very intentional—in the way they look, in their singular focus, how the helpful content is choreographed and in their ultimate goal—to get readers to take action and become your customer.

Shooks are faster to create, easier to read and are designed according to an intentional and proven direct response marketing formula. This is an important and critical differentiator from all the other types of books out there because direct response books are focused on getting readers to <u>respond</u> (not just read and put on their bookshelf).

As I've previously mentioned, "shook" is short (no pun intended) for "<u>s</u>hort, <u>h</u>elpful b<u>ook</u>." It is my trademarked description of a specific book format I have perfected, which has a specific goal, content structure, physical size and page count. You can create print, digital and audio shooks.

With this in mind, let me describe some of the reasons why I think shooks are special and the ideal type of book for you to create if you are looking to attract new customers.

Shooks Invite Readership

Since the most obvious difference between a typical printed standard business book and a shook is the size, let me start by describing what makes a shook, a shook. Printed shooks are professionally printed, perfect bound paperback books. They are similar in quality to the types of books you buy on Amazon or at a local bookstore, and they are designed and formatted by professional book cover and interior designers, so they look and feel great.

Rather than the 5.5"x8.5" or 6"x9" trim size of typical business books, most shooks are intentionally designed to be 5.06"x7.81" in size, making them slightly smaller, and therefore, different looking than other books. This size creates a "pattern interrupt" when you hand a prospect your shook because it's different from what they are used to. Today, appearing new, fresh and different is a smart strategy to get noticed, which is why shooks are designed the way they are.

Instead of the *"There is no way I am going to read that"* response many people have when they get a standard book, a shook's size invites them to read.

This smaller size also makes your shook easy to carry, share with others, mail and display. I keep several copies of my shooks in my car and in my laptop bag, so I always have them on hand to give away when I meet business owners and potential prospects for my business. My shooks are my business cards.

Shooks Are Physically Easier to Read

Shooks are designed to be physically easier to read. I don't know about you, but as I get older, reading printed text either on paper or on a screen is getting harder.

Most designers do not worry about the physical readability of books, marketing and advertising materials, which is a big mistake. Instead of using design criteria and typography that are easier on the eye, they use a hard-to-read layout and hard-to-read fonts. Remember, if a person cannot easily read your content, there is a high probability he or she will simply give up trying.

For years, I have been preaching about the importance of making everything you create easy to physically read. As a side note, if you visit my blog at **MikeCapuzzi.com** and search on *"readability,"* you will find many articles and examples where I discuss the importance of making your marketing material easy on the eyes.

The design of the words you are reading at this very moment are not just some default setting we merely used. The font choice, size and line spacing I am using in *The Magic of Short Books* are the result of a study I did with people on my email list, where I asked them to review eight different standard book font and line spacing combinations.

What you are seeing on these pages is the #1 "easiest to read" shook design layout. The good news is if you work with me, you don't have to worry about all these details. I take care of everything.

Shooks Are Faster to Read

Most business books have 30,000–50,000 words, with many exceeding 75,000 words. They tend to be at least 200 pages and often can reach 400 pages. They take the average reader days, if not weeks, to read, and while my bookshelf is filled with these traditional types of business books, I wanted shooks to be different. I am not saying the world doesn't need these types of longer books; I am saying most business owners would be better served publishing a shook instead of a book.

Shooks contain 10,000–18,000 words total and have 80–140 pages, but these are smaller pages, so they are faster to read and can be read by an average-speed reader in an hour or two. This means you can have an hour or two of "quiet time" with your readers, where they are focused on your message and getting to know you and how you can help them better.

Shooks Are Focused

Shooks are written for a specific and targeted reader, typically the type of person who would be an ideal customer for your business, and if you could wave a magic wand, you would be able to find hundreds if not thousands of similar people.

If you decide to personally work with me to develop your shook, one of the first things we will work on together is the identification of the reader you want to attract, help and eventually turn into a customer. This is a critical first step and one that provides a framework for the shook's content and promotion.

Shooks Are Easier to Understand

Shooks are helpful bite sized chunks of information your target reader is looking for. They are not meant to be the "complete and final" word on a topic. Instead, they contain highly focused content that offers helpful information, insights, tips, ideas, etc., on a topic.

Rather than teach a reader everything about the topic, shooks enlighten readers with your unique knowledge, expertise and opinions and then extend an invitation to get more from you as part of the "next step." If your subject requires lengthy text, my suggestion is to consider a series of shooks instead of one long, traditional book.

Shooks Provide Undivided Attention

When expertly crafted, which it will be when we work together, a shook provides about an hour or so of focused "conversation" with your readers because you are helping them with a specific topic they want help with.

By providing this laser-focused message and related content, you are practically guaranteed your targeted ideal reader will devour your shook, cover to cover. This means you have their undivided attention and focus on you and your message.

The benefits of this undivided attention?

- Increased name recognition

- Enhanced reputation

- Boosted believability

- Deeper trust

- More transparency

- Established authority (notice how the word "authority" starts with the word "author?)

What other marketing media do you use that has these types of big benefits?

Shooks Offer Additional Information

Shooks are interactive and have various opportunities for readers to get valuable bonuses and extend the power of the shook with free online content (you have seen me do this throughout this shook). This allows readers to get more helpful information and gives you the opportunity to capture their contact information, thereby building a follow-up database.

Shooks Get Readers to Raise Their Hand

Shooks have a clear "next step" call-to-action to get interested readers to self-identify. When people read your shook, there's a high probability you will have intrigued them and provided value and reason to take the next step, whatever that is for your sales process. Working together, we will uncover this next step and incorporate it clearly in your shook.

Let's Get Your Shook Started!

I hope you are getting as excited about the possibility of authoring your own shook as I am about you joining the ranks of being a shook author. I truly believe that creating a shook will become one of the most prized and profitable money-making assets in your business. Schedule a Shook Strategy Session with me by visiting **BiteSizedBooks.com**.

SHOOK IN ACTION

Title:	*Million Dollar Fitness Secrets*
Author:	Amir Siddiqui
Shook hook:	Discover the fitness secrets from Dubai's highest paid personal trainer
Page count:	104
Active CTA:	Schedule an initial fitness session
Passive CTA:	Download The Symmetry Method, his 12 week exercise and diet program for free

CHAPTER 3

THE ALCHEMY OF SHOOKS

What I am about to share is the formula you should use for "constructing" your shook. It's what I use to author my shooks, and it's what I use for my shook clients. There is no need to reinvent the wheel here. Just make sure you follow the steps I outline and ensure your shook contains the required building blocks I am about to share.

Before you start the content creation phase of your shook, there is a necessary and required planning phase. This is where you give serious thought about your shook goals, your ideal reader, the big idea/promise of your shook, your calls-to-action and your publishing options.

After you identify and articulate the foundational building blocks, you can move on to the content blocks. The content blocks are focused on the four essential parts of a shook, with each part containing a set of shook building blocks specific to that part.

By thinking in terms of these four essential parts of your shook, you will be able to quickly and easily complete the content for each part. When I work with an individual shook client, my initial coaching calls are broken down and focus on each of these parts. The end results are clarity and a simple and straight-forward path to getting the shook done.

Essential Parts of Your Shook

1. The Cover Content

2. The Front Matter Content

3. The Main Matter Content

4. The Back Matter Content

What follows are each of the building blocks and what you need to think about. I go into greater detail on many of these building blocks and how to expand upon them in this shook's next part, From Wish to Published.

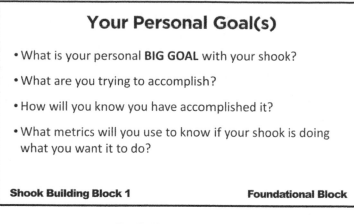

Building Block 1
Your Personal Goal(s)

You need to know right from the outset what your primary goal of your shook is, and if you've read this far, you know it's not about selling it!

What are you looking to accomplish with your shook, and how will you know you have accomplished it? Most business owners I work with want to use their shook for two primary reasons:

1. To increase their influence and authority

2. To attract more of their ideal customers

What are your goals for your shook?

Your Goal(s) for Your Readers

1. Help them.

2. What do you want your readers to <u>achieve</u> after reading your shook?

3. What do you want your readers to <u>do</u> after reading your shook?

Shook Building Block 2   **Foundational Block**

Building Block 2
Your Goal(s) for Your Readers

In addition to your own personal goals, you want to identify the goals you have for your readers. The first one is obvious; you want to help them with the main reason they are reading your shook. This is the concept of helping before selling.

But what do you want them to do next?

This next step is critically important to your shook and requires critical thought.

Identify Your Ideal Reader

- Identify your ideal reader.

- This should be your eventual ideal customer/client/patient.

- List any important demographics, psychographics, details we should keep in mind when crafting the book's content.

- If you can focus on one "type" of reader, the better.

Shook Building Block 3   **Foundational Block**

Building Block 3
Identify Your Ideal Reader

The first step to outlining your shook is to identify your ideal targeted reader. Who do you want to read this book and become a customer?

This is the person you write your shook for and nobody else! Everything on and in your shook should be designed and written for this person so that when they get a copy they say to themselves, "This book was written for me!"

This is a critical, must-do first step, so consider your ideal target reader carefully.

Your Shook Hook

- What is the BIG IDEA or BIG PROMISE with your shook?

- How are you trying to help your readers?

- Why should anybody read your shook?

  —What BIG problem will your shook start to fix for your reader?

Shook Building Block 4   **Foundational Block**

Building Block 4
Your Shook Hook

The hook of your shook is the Big Idea/Promise behind it and the reason you created the shook for your ideal and targeted reader.

Create a promise for your shook and explain to your reader how investing the time to read it will help them solve a problem or gain something they want. Remember, nobody wants to read your shook until they understand what it's going to do for them and how it's going to make their life easier, better, etc.

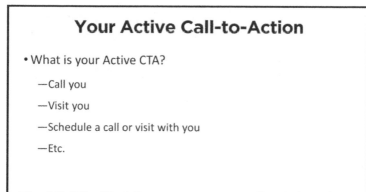

Your Active Call-to-Action

- What is your Active CTA?

  —Call you

  —Visit you

  —Schedule a call or visit with you

  —Etc.

Shook Building Block 5　　　　　　　　**Foundational Block**

Building Block 5
Your Active Call-to-Action

At a minimum, shooks have two different, direct response mechanisms and pathways in them. The first one is the "active pathway," which is for the person who reads the shook and immediately wants to take the next step as outlined in the shook. In the case of this shook, it would be the reader who knows she wants to craft a shook and she schedules a Shook Strategy Session with me.

This is accomplished via the Active Call-to-Action, which again in my case is to schedule a call with me. Other shook authors may want to invite readers to visit their place of business, call or schedule a call or visit.

Your Passive Call-to-Action

- What is your Passive CTA?
- What *new pain* have you created you can solve with additional information that can be watched, read or downloaded?
  - —Tip sheet
  - —Report
  - —Video
  - —Etc.

Shook Building Block 6   **Foundational Block**

Building Block 6
Your Passive Call-to-Action

Reality means not all shook readers will be ready for the active pathway and will need more information and engagement in order to respond to the Active Call-to-Action. For these readers, we provide the "passive pathway," which is an interim step that allows them to get more information from you in return for their contact information.

This Passive Call-to-Action could be a simple download like a tip sheet, report, video, etc. It should be some additional helpful information that readers will want and are willing to exchange their information for. Smart shook authors will then follow up with marketing strategies to stay connected.

Publishing Options—Book Printer

• Option 1-Book printer benefits:

—You control ALL distribution, sales and fulfillment of your shook.

—You can order batches of printed shooks as needed, however, for best shipping, you typically need to order at least 100 copies.

—This option is typically the best choice for the person who doesn't want /need their book on Amazon.

Shook Building Block 7   **Foundational Block**

Building Block 7
Publishing Options—Book Printer

There are two primary ways shooks get printed—using a book printer or using Amazon's Kindle Direct Publishing (KDP). For most local business owners who only want to be "five mile famous" (meaning they are only using their shooks in their local community), using a book printer is the preferred choice. This option allows you to control all distribution of your shooks and you can order them in small batches as you need them.

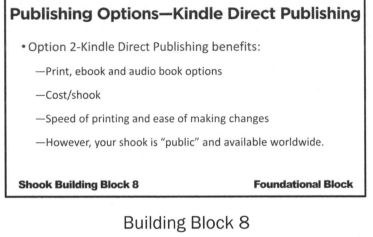

Publishing Options—Kindle Direct Publishing

- Option 2-Kindle Direct Publishing benefits:
  - —Print, ebook and audio book options
  - —Cost/shook
  - —Speed of printing and ease of making changes
  - —However, your shook is "public" and available worldwide.

Shook Building Block 8   **Foundational Block**

Building Block 8
Publishing Options—Kindle Direct Publishing

Kindle Direct Publishing is Amazon's author platform and allows you to get your shook out to the entire world. For business owners who have a global audience or reach, this is typically the way you want to distribute your shook. Amazon's book printing prices are typically cheaper than traditional book printers, and it's easy to make changes to your shook when it's on Amazon.

If you go the KDP route, just realize that your shook is public, and anybody can purchase it.

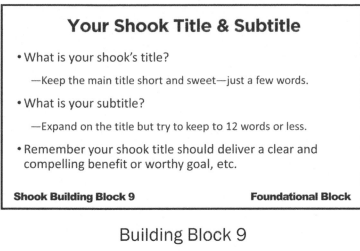

Your Shook Title & Subtitle

• What is your shook's title?

　—Keep the main title short and sweet—just a few words.

• What is your subtitle?

　—Expand on the title but try to keep to 12 words or less.

• Remember your shook title should deliver a clear and compelling benefit or worthy goal, etc.

Shook Building Block 9　　　　　　　**Foundational Block**

Building Block 9
Your Shook Title & Subtitle

Crafting your shook's title and subtitle is an iterative and important process. It's similar to developing a strong headline when copywriting and requires time, work and rework to get it right.

The good news is if you've identified your targeted reader and your hook, creating an attention-grabbing title that practically forces people to want to read your shook is simple.

Personally, I am a fan of a short title and longer subtitle. Take a look at the cover of this shook to see an example of a good title that took several rounds of ideas to finalize.

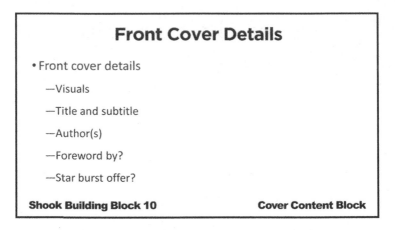

Building Block 10
Front Cover Details

Your shook's front cover is like an artist's canvas. It's where you get the opportunity to make a powerful first impression, and unless you are a graphic designer yourself, you want to let a professional create your shook cover.

Using the right graphics, fonts and other details is critically important, and you don't want to be sloppy or cheap about this. You also don't need to spend thousands of dollars on the cover either. Every business owner who works with me will get a professionally designed cover that will get the attention of your target reader and make your shook look great!

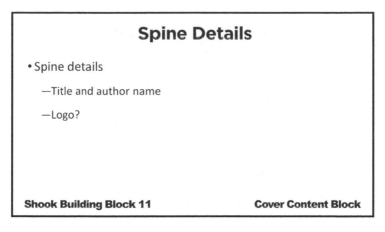

Building Block 11
Spine Details

Don't laugh, but you need to consider what you want to have on your shook's spine, so that when it's sitting on a bookshelf, it can be easily identified.

Unlike many typical lead generation books, which are too small, shooks meet the minimum requirement in order to have text on the spine so that it looks like any other professionally printed book.

Typically, you only want to have your title, possibly the subtitle and your name on the spine. If there is room available, consider adding your logo on it, too. Your goal is to make it easy to find your shook on a bookshelf.

Back Cover Details

• Back cover details

—Price (and book category if selling by retail)

—Reason to read headline

—Book description and "what's inside" bullets

—Author bio and website URL

—ISBN and barcode (if selling via Amazon or other retailers)

Shook Building Block 12   **Cover Content Block**

Building Block 12
Back Cover Details

The back cover is the final piece of the three parts of your shook cover (front, spine and back). Here is what I like to include on the back cover:

- Price and book category.

- Strong *reason to read* headline.

- Short book description, including specific "here's what's inside" bullets.

- A short author bio and website.

- ISBN and barcode (if selling on Amazon or other online retailers).

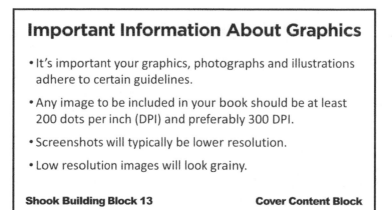

Building Block 13
Important Information About Graphics

This building block is a critical reminder about the importance of using high-quality, high-resolution graphics in your shook. Because it's a printed book, it's best if all your photographs, graphics and illustrations are at a minimum 200 dots per inch (DPI) and preferably 300 DPI.

Unfortunately, this is not always possible, and just realize that lower quality graphics will not print as clear and may look a bit grainy.

Reader Bonus/Gift Offer

- This is your shook's "Passive Call-to-Action" and is the secondary action you want a reader to take.

- This one-page offer is designed to give the reader a valuable bonus/gift if they visit your website and exchange their contact information for free gift or call your business.

- This should be something of value that the reader would want.

- The offer should include a simple web URL for the reader to visit or phone number to call.

Shook Building Block 14   **Front Matter Block**

Building Block 14 (& 32)
Reader Bonus/Gift Offer Page

We've finally gotten to the first page of your shook. This is the right-hand side page that is first seen when somebody opens your shook. In many books this page is left blank or is the title page. In a shook this page is specifically designed to be a reader bonus/gift page where readers can get a valuable bonus/gift right away (see Building Block #6).

I also like to repeat this page as the very last even page in a shook (Building Block 32).

Also By Page

- OPTIONAL

- If you have written/created other books, reports, trainings, etc., you should include them on this page.

Shook Building Block 15   **Front Matter Block**

Building Block 15
Also By Page

This is an optional page, but if you've created other books, reports, trainings, etc., you should include them on this page.

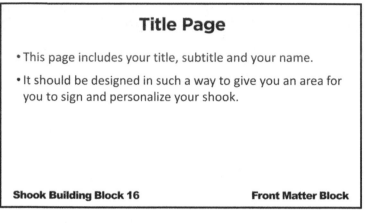

Building Block 16
Title Page

Your title page includes your title, subtitle and name. I like to design this page so that it leaves room for you to write a personal note and sign your shooks when giving them out.

Testimonial Page(s)

• **OPTIONAL**

• If you want to distribute pre-release copies of your shook to your inner circle, important people you know, customers, etc., for them to send you a shook testimonial you would include them on these pages.

• Testimonials should inspire others to read your shook.

• They should be short, sweet and specific.

Shook Building Block 17   **Front Matter Block**

Building Block 17
Testimonial Page(s)

This is an optional page, but if you have testimonials and reviews of your shook, you should include them here. The way you get them is to give out prerelease copies to specific individuals and ask them to write a short testimonial about the shook. Be strategic about who you ask to review.

My shook client, Doug Brown, got a former client to become a current client again by simply asking him to review his shook. This wasn't their intention, but after reading the shook, the former client realized what he was missing and signed back up for his program.

Copyright Page

- Copyright ownership—typically you or your business name.
- Publisher information
  —Optionally you can use your company or brand as the publisher.
- Any important legal information and disclaimers.
- Consider adding a date code to track shook versions.

Shook Building Block 18   **Front Matter Block**

Building Block 18
Copyright Page

This page includes all copyright information, disclaimers, publisher details and important legal information.

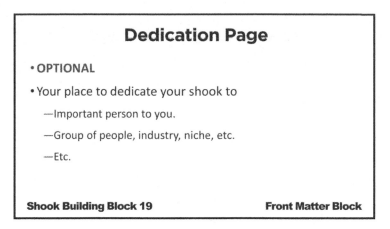

Building Block 19
Dedication Page

This is an optional page which allows you to dedicate your shook to an important person or persons, a group of people, specific niche, etc.

Acknowledgments Page

- OPTIONAL

- Your place to acknowledge people who helped you.

Shook Building Block 20   **Front Matter Block**

Building Block 20
Acknowledgments Page

This is an optional page, which allows you to acknowledge and thank people who were helpful to you in creating your shook.

Table of Contents

- A Table of Contents is important to have and one of the most important parts of a nonfiction book.

- Your section and chapter headings should be clear and inform the reader what's in store.

- A good table of contents tells the story of your shook.

Shook Building Block 21   **Front Matter Block**

Building Block 21
Table of Contents

The table of contents is an important part of your shook and should entice readers to want to read it. Make sure you check and double-check the titles and page numbers are correct before going to print.

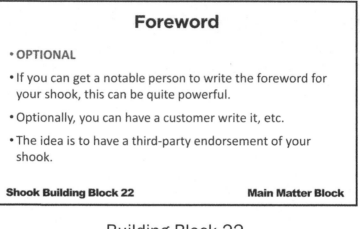

Foreword

- **OPTIONAL**

- If you can get a notable person to write the foreword for your shook, this can be quite powerful.

- Optionally, you can have a customer write it, etc.

- The idea is to have a third-party endorsement of your shook.

Shook Building Block 22   **Main Matter Block**

Building Block 22
Foreword

This is an optional page, but if it makes sense and you can find a V.I.P. to write the foreword to your shook, it can make it that much more powerful. When thinking about a person to write it, consider who you would like to have associated with your shook and who may be inclined to share it with their circles of influence simply because they were asked to write the foreword.

If you cannot find a notable V.I.P., consider asking a valuable customer to write it for you.

Who Should Read This Book?

• **OPTIONAL**

• If you want to connect even more, while also repelling others, you can include this section where you are specific about who should read the book (and who shouldn't).

• This is a bold strategy, but it can strengthen the bond with your target reader.

Shook Building Block 23   **Main Matter Block**

Building Block 23
Who Should Read This Book?

This an optional section but one I personally like to include, like I did in this shook. I like to be upfront and transparent with my shook's goals and exactly who I created it for. While I appreciate people who are interested in my shook, if they don't fit the profile of the types of business owners I'm looking to attract and work with, they do me little good.

This section allows me to boldly proclaim who should and should not read my shook. In turn this will strengthen the bond with my target readers, since they know I wrote it specifically for them.

My Promise to You

• OPTIONAL

• Starting your shook off with a bold promise is smart.

• It keeps you focused on exactly what you need to convey in the shook and reminds you of its purpose.

• It prepares your reader for what to expect in the pages to come and sets an important tone on how you conduct your business.

Shook Building Block 24   **Main Matter Block**

Building Block 24
My Promise to You

This is an optional page but one I believe you should include. Starting your shook off with a bold promise is a smart way to keep you focused on what you must deliver and prepare your readers for what to expect. So few business owners set any sort of lofty expectation these days, so making a promise from the beginning shows you are different than the masses.

Introduction

- Reason why intro.
- Here's what you'll discover in this shook.
- Here's why this is different.
- Why this is important to you now.
- Personal invitation to contact you.

Shook Building Block 25   **Main Matter Block**

Building Block 25
Introduction

I recommend all shook authors start their shook with a "reason why" introduction, which articulates the reason(s) why you are publishing it. Let your readers know what they will get by reading it, why it's different, and why it's important they read it now.

An excellent book recommendation for crafting your "why" is *Start with Why* by Simon Sinek. I found this book to be an excellent reminder when creating any type of marketing message.

Content Chapters #1-#7

- Each of these content chapters is the main content of your shook.

- These chapters are typically 1,500-2,500 words in length.

- Consider ending with a chapter-specific call-to-action.

  —Call or visit you or include some valuable thing for the reader to get with no opt-in.

Shook Building Block 26　　　　　　　　　**Main Matter Block**

Building Block 26
Content Chapters

These are the main content pages of your shook. Remember, shooks are short books that are NOT designed to teach readers everything you know about the topic of the shook. They are meant to provide valuable information and then guide the reader to the next step, which is typically contacting you.

I like to target 5-7 main content chapters, but based on your specific shook, you may have more. If you work with me, we will figure this out early on, so you know exactly what is needed. What is important is the structure of each chapter and the option to offer additional valuable information with a chapter-specific download.

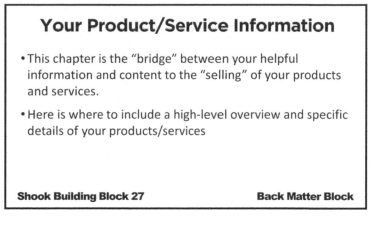

Your Product/Service Information

- This chapter is the "bridge" between your helpful information and content to the "selling" of your products and services.

- Here is where to include a high-level overview and specific details of your products/services

Shook Building Block 27   **Back Matter Block**

Building Block 27
Your Product/Service Information

This chapter is an important transitional chapter from your Main Matter content into the Back Matter where you are now "selling." You should provide a high-level overview of how you can help readers achieve what they are looking for and align your products/services with their wants and needs.

The Next Step

- What is the "one thing" you want the reader to do?

- This is your "Active Call-to-Action" and the main thing you want a reader to do after reading your shook.

  —Typically call your place of business or visit.

- Give explicit and detailed instructions on what to do next.

Shook Building Block 28   **Back Matter Block**

Building Block 28
The Next Step

It's critical your shook tells readers the next thing they must do in order to achieve the goal they were seeking when they first picked it up. I call this the "Active Call-to-Action," and it's the thing you want the reader to do after reading your shook.

I like to keep this limited to one thing, so it's clear and simple to do. Depending on your business, it could be to call you, visit you, fill out a survey, etc.

Give explicit and detailed instructions on what to do next if they truly want to solve their problem or achieve their goal.

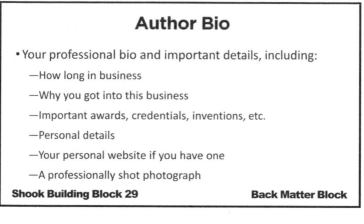

Building Block 29
Author Bio

Include your bio and important details about your background, experience, etc. This allows your readers to get to know you better.

If you don't have professionally shot photographs and headshot photos, now is a good time to get them done. You can use one on your back cover and in your bio.

Frequently Asked Questions

- **OPTIONAL**

- If you have many frequently asked questions about your products and services, consider including the top ones in your shook.

Shook Building Block 30   **Back Matter Block**

Building Block 30
Frequently Asked Questions

This is an optional section, but if you have many typical questions prospects ask you, including them in your shook is helpful.

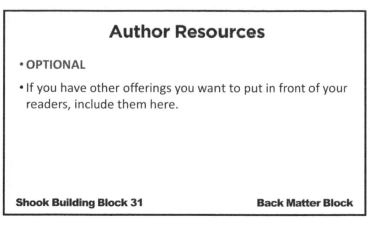

Building Block 31
Author Resources

This is an optional page, but if you have other resources you would like readers to know about, include them in this page.

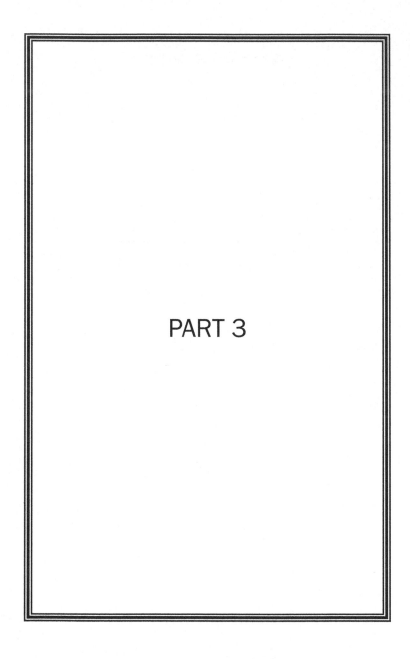

PART 3

FROM WISH TO PUBLISHED

SHOOK IN ACTION

Title:	*Sleep Better*
Author:	Jeff Giagnocavo
Shook hook:	Practical tips and strategies to get a better night's sleep
Page count:	100
Active CTA:	Visit their store and receive a free pillow
Passive CTA:	None

CHAPTER 4

WHICH TYPE OF BUSINESS OWNER ARE YOU?

In all my years of helping business owners leverage the power of short, helpful books and become published "Main Street Authors," I have come to realize there are two distinct types of business owners.

The first are those who only dream about being a published author without ever taking any action to make it happen.

The second are those who are ready to act when the opportunity presents itself.

Many people will tell you they want to become an author and write a book, but we both know very few actually make it happen. It's the nature of people— the classic tale of the willful and the wishful.

Most people will keep dreaming, while the few who are serious about becoming a published author and becoming a significant, respected and valued expert in their community will take action.

My goal for you with writing *The Magic of Short Books* is to show you a better type of book to create for your business and then show you exactly how to do it.

With this latter goal in mind, the next few chapters give you a set of practical and fairly easy strategies to get your shook done. I am holding nothing back and giving you my entire blueprint for creating a powerful and profitable short, helpful book.

CHAPTER 5

HOW TO AUTHOR YOUR SHOOK

The key to authoring a shook that will position you as an expert authority and attract more ideal customers for your business is to take some time and give thoughtful consideration to what you are trying to accomplish. I'm not suggesting you invest weeks or months "planning" your shook, but you do need to spend a few hours thinking this through. To help you with this process, I have identified six key elements to authoring your shook. Going through these and using them to plan your shook will give you a powerful fast start.

1. Your Goals

Like any worthwhile business and marketing effort, you should start by thinking about and articulating your goals for the project. Specific to your shook, there are two types of goals you should consider before you start.

The first are your own personal goals you want to achieve with your shook. Consider these questions:

- *What is your big goal with your shook?*

- *What is the #1 thing you want to accomplish?*

- *How will you know you have accomplished it?*

- *What metrics will you use to know if your shook is doing what you want it to do?*

The second are your goals for your targeted reader. Consider these questions:

- *What do you want your readers to achieve after reading your shook?*

- *What do you want your readers to do next?*

2. Identify Your Ideal Reader

It's important to have a clear picture of an ideal reader so you can work on authoring content that will attract as many as possible while simultaneously repelling those who do not fit your ideal reader profile. You should author your shook for the type of person who is a great customer for you and who you want to serve.

You need to think about this person and what they want/need and craft your shook's content to give them both.

Remember, your ideal reader wants:

- To learn more about you/your business and how you can specifically help them.

- To get something they crave.

- To reduce pain, expenses, wasted time, etc.

- To gain pleasure, health, time, money, comfort, happiness, etc.

- A trustworthy authority to give him or her a simple and clear path to getting all this.

3. Your Shook Hook

Your shook hook is a single, big idea and reason why your shook exists. Your shook hook should:

- Be emotionally stirring and wake him/her up.

- Be easy to understand.

- Sound new, unique, original and break through the noise and clutter.

- Be instantly appealing (to your ideal reader).

- Connect the dots to your product/service.

To help you develop your shook's hook, consider these questions about your ideal reader:

- *What is keeping them awake at night?*

- *What are they mad about?*

- *What do they desire the most?*

Your readers want simplicity and clarity. Do your best to make it specific and simple to understand.

4. Your Shook Title

The title (and subtitle) of your shook is a critical aspect of authoring your shook. An effective, attention-grabbing title will make your shook irresistible to your ideal reader, whereas a poor title will fall flat.

Coming up with a great title is typically an iterative process that takes time and consideration. Do not rush this process. Personally, I prefer simple and direct titles and more detailed subtitles. I like to try to keep the title short and sweet and then expand on it more with a subtitle. Here are a few of my clients' titles/subtitles:

Medicare Made to Order: A New and Exciting Way to Think About Medicare and Get the Benefits You Deserve

Are Your Teeth Toxic?: What Your Dentist Never Told You About Mercury in Your Silver Fillings

Million Dollar Fitness Secrets: Proven Methods from Dubai's Highest Paid Personal Trainer

The Magic of Tradeshowmanship: How to Ace Your Next Event!

You're Not Alone: Living with Dementia

Who's Stealing Your Retirement? 7 Cunning Thieves Who Are Trying to Ransack Your Nest Egg (and How You Can Catch 'Em)

As you think about your title, keep these do's and do not's in mind.

Do:

- Make a promise of a benefit.

- Be simple and direct.

- Target an audience and use their language.

- Use metaphors, alliteration, popular phrases.

Do not:

- Rush this process.

- Use "special report type" titles (e.g., hype).

- Forget how important your title is!

5. Your Calls-to-Action

In my experience, not providing simple ways for readers to either get more information from you or connect with you is one of the biggest mistakes I see authors make. Your shook is a conversation starter. In order to keep this conversation moving forward, you must offer at least two different pathways for readers to take after they read your shook:

1. Your Active Call-to-Action.

2. Your Passive Call-to-Action.

Your shook's Active Call-to-Action is the #1 thing you want readers to do after reading your shook. For most shook authors, it is one of these main things:

- Call you or visit you.

- Schedule a call or visit with you.

- Participate at an event or seminar.

- Take an assessment.

In this case of the shook you are now reading, my Active Call-to-Action is to schedule a Shook Strategy Session with me to brainstorm your shook and see if working together is a good idea.

Your shook's Passive Call-to-Action is the secondary action you want a reader to take and is designed for you to collect email contact information in return for additional helpful information. What simple and easy-to-digest information do you have that readers will want? This could be a tip sheet, action plan, a "lost chapter," additional training, etc.

One smart strategy to think about here is what *new problem* have you created for your reader and then offer a fix for that problem with your Passive Call-to-Action.

6. Your Main Content

The structure and flow of your shook's main content is important, and you must keep in mind that your objective is NOT to create the complete A to Z book on your subject matter but instead offer bite-sized chunks of helpful information.

Unlike traditional-length books, your shook only requires 8,000–12,000 words of main content broken into short chapters. My suggestion is to aim for seven main chapters if you can.

As far as ways to write the main content, here are several strategies for authoring it. These are in order of my personal preference.

WRITE IT—the traditional method of writing your shook's content is, in my opinion, the best way to create your shook if you enjoy writing and are decent at it. I get that it can feel like a daunting task, but I believe sitting down and actually writing your content will pay off in many different ways in your business.

You will see holes in your messaging and develop new and better ways to describe your solutions. No other person is as passionate and interested in your topic as you are, so if you can set time aside and use this shook as your blueprint, I know you can do it.

I literally shut myself in my office for a few days and crafted most of the content for this shook. Of course, I had properly outlined my thoughts and planned before sequestering myself, but I was able to complete most of this shook's content in a single, focused day. I am not saying you need to do the same thing, but there is something powerful about getting away from your day-to-day distractions to make yourself exceptionally productive.

Another option is to commit to writing 750 words a day, five days a week. Again, if you have properly outlined and planned your shook, this strategy will take you about five weeks to complete your shook content by only writing 750 words a day, five days a week. You should be able to craft 750 words in about 30–60 minutes, and on certain days you may be able to write 1,000 or even 1,500 words effortlessly. The more you write, the easier it becomes.

PRESENT IT—if you do face-to-face presentations or even virtual webinar-based talks, your 60-minute presentation could make the perfect content for your shook. The skills necessary to craft a compelling presentation, including the flow and content, are the same skills needed to create a good shook. Essentially, you deliver your presentation, record it and then have it transcribed so that it can be edited into its final format.

TALK IT—another book-authoring strategy that is popular these days is to talk your book out on your smart phone or computer, have it transcribed and then polished by a professional writer. For some, it might be easier to talk your shook out instead of sitting down at a computer. There are several online services for transcription, which make this once expensive and tedious task much easier.

TIP: Check out **Rev.com** for a service I use.

REPURPOSE IT—if you have lots of content you've previously written, you can repurpose it for your shook, saving you hours of time and energy. For example, if you have been writing blog content for years, you can take selected blog posts and use them as the main content of your shook. You could also convert videos and podcasts you have recorded into useable content.

HIRE IT—a final strategy and one I used to create *Dream Inc.*, was to find and hire a professional ghostwriter to interview each of the 31 contributors and write their chapter based on the interview content. You could hire a ghostwriter to interview you and write your shook's content.

Proofreading and Copyediting

When your shook's manuscript is finished, it's important you have it proofread and copyedited by an experienced set of eyes. While it's almost impossible to publish any type of book that has no errors in it, you do want to do your best to minimize grammar and content mistakes, which is why you need to find an experienced copyeditor/proofreader to review your manuscript.

If you don't have this type of resource, visit Upwork.com or Guru.com and do a search. Just make sure the person you hire is experienced and performs quality work.

"What If I Don't Have Enough Content?"

In order to have text on the spine of your shook's cover, you typically need a minimum of 100 pages. To me, having text on the spine is critical for having a "real book," and I always aim for this page count. If you find you are short on pages, consider adding:

- Blank notes pages.

- Photos & images.

- Quotes and testimonials.

- Third-party content, articles, tips, etc.

- Increase font size, line-spacing, margins, etc.

CHAPTER 6

HOW TO DESIGN
YOUR SHOOK

O nce your shook's manuscript is finished and copyedited, the next step is to complete the interior and cover design. In my opinion, a poorly designed book is worse than not having any book at all, and I have seen countless self-published books that look like they were put together by a fourth grader.

If you are going to go through the effort of writing a quality shook, the last thing you want to do is have it reflect poorly on you because you did not adhere to book design best practices. There are two critical shook design principles you must follow for creating a quality shook:

1. An eye-catching and effective cover design.

2. A clean, easy-to-read interior design.

While both of these may sound simple for you to do yourself, I strongly advise you to seek out the help of an experienced cover and interior designer. If you decide to work with me, we will take care of all this for you. Otherwise you can find goo designers on **Upwork.com** and **Guru.com**. You can also check out **99designs.com** and create a cover contest where multiple designers will send you cover ideas.

Cover Design Tips

I always start by browsing through **Amazon.com** and seeing what other similar books look like to try to get ideas for a shook cover. This way you can make suggestions and show your designer the type of cover you want and give him or her a good starting point.

Some covers are text-only, and others rely heavily on photographs and graphics. Your shook's focus, target reader and business branding should ultimately decide on the design direction of your cover. Here are a few important tips:

- Don't be cheap about your cover design!

- Work with an experienced cover designer.

- If using graphics, photos or illustrations on the cover, make sure they are high resolution.

Check out the second module in the bonus training I am giving you with this shook. It goes into greater detail on how to design your shook. Get it at **ReaderBonus.com/tmsb**.

Interior Design Tips

Good effective book design follows timeless design and readability rules. I can always spot a book that was designed by the author or an inexperienced designer because it breaks these rules and looks amateurish. Good interior book design can range from simple, text-only design to highly designed books with full page graphics, callouts and other graphic enhancements. Of course, the type of look you want will dictate the cost of the design.

For the shooks we publish, I like to keep things simple and focused more on readability instead of trying to be fancy. Making your shook as easy on the eyes as possible is critical, especially for certain age demographics. Be careful of using fancy fonts or too many fonts and watch your type size.

The interior design rules I am using in this shook are the result of several readability tests I conducted a few years ago with this design being a clear front-runner. Here is what we are using:

- Title font—Franklin Gothic Book @ 20 pt.

- Body font—Georgia Pro @ 11 pt.

- Line spacing—1.3sp and 1pt after paragraphs.

- Inside, outside, top and bottom margins—0.85", 0.5", 1.0", 0.8".

- Justified text.

There are several ways you can design the interior of your shook with my #1 recommendation being to work with an experienced book interior designer. Other alternatives include:

- Do-it-yourself book interior design templates. The folks at **BookDesignTemplates.com** offer some nice DIY options.

- Do-it-yourself software tools (Scrivener, Kindle Create).

When it comes to designing your shook's interior and cover, you have several options available, but in my professional opinion, there is really only one choice that makes sense—assuming you want a shook to be proud of when displaying and giving to prospective customers.

WORK WITH A BOOK DESIGN PRO!

Like with anything in life, you only get one chance to make a good first impression and an incorrectly designed shook is worse than no shook at all. So please keep that in mind as you consider your shook's interior and cover design.

CHAPTER 7

HOW TO PUBLISH YOUR SHOOK

B efore I jump into the various options you have to publish your shook, I want to start by describing the different shook formats that are available to you. Which formats you decide to leverage should be based on the ways your ideal targeted reader consumes information. I suggest you use as many of these formats as possible so you can ensure your shook is available in all the different ways your prospects consume books.

Printed Shook

The primary, default format for a shook is the printed, paperback version. As a reminder, all shooks are slightly different in size (5.06"x7.81") and are printed either by a book printer or **Amazon.com**. Printed shooks are the most versatile and effective format for Main Street business owners and offer you many different ways to use (at events, in direct mail, in your place of business, etc.).

As far as getting your shook printed, you essentially have two options. You can use an "on-demand" book printer and/or you can use **Amazon.com**. If your audience is local, I recommend simply printing your shook with a book printer and keeping copies in your office for distribution and use.

On-demand book printers allow you to print as few as one book or as many as you want. I typically recommend ordering in batches of 100 so that you don't have boxes of shooks sitting around. Some recommended book printers include **Steuben-Press.com** and **48HourBooks.com**.

If you have a global audience or want to tap into the distribution power of Amazon, you can do so by publishing your shook via Amazon's Kindle Direct Publishing (KDP) Program. This enables you to sell your shook in Amazon's vast network and also allows you to order "author copies" at a steeply discounted price. Check out **KDP.Amazon.com** for details.

PDF Shook

Creating a PDF version of your shook is easy and allows you to offer your entire shook or just a few chapters via your website, email and social media. If you decide to create a PDF shook, make sure you add a table of contents that has clickable links and save it in "book mode" in Adobe Acrobat. Your book designer should be able to do this for you.

Flip Shook

A "flip" shook is a format I use, and we create for our clients. You can see an example of a flip shook at **BiteSizedBooks.com/authors**. If you visit that link, you will see you can literally page through the shook like you would with the printed version. This format also allows you to have a clickable Table of Contents so readers can navigate your shook easily. We use Flip Builder (**FlipBuilder.com**) to create these.

Kindle & eBook Shook

Kindle and other eBooks are a popular option for many consumers, and you may want to consider offering this format. There are two primary eBook formats—MOBI for Kindle books and ePub for most other eBook readers. The process to create these formats is much more complicated than it should be in my opinion, and it's definitely not something you want to tackle on your own. Make sure you hire an experienced eBook designer to turn your printed shook into a properly designed eBook. We offer this service to our shook publishing clients.

Audio Shook

Audio books are another popular format for people to "read" books, and services like Audible, Amazon and iTunes allow you to distribute your audio shook.

You can also create your own MP3 format for your own distribution use. If you decide to go this route, you can either record your own audio shook yourself (just make sure it is a high-quality recording) or hire a professional voiceover artist. We offer this service to our shook clients, and if you are doing it yourself, check out ACX (**ACX.com**) to get started.

CHAPTER 8

HOW TO LEVERAGE
YOUR SHOOK

Shooks are without a doubt one of the most versatile assets a business owner can create for his or her business. They can be used for lead generation, event marketing, referral marketing, local news and PR, etc. I have heard from more than one client that their best customers and clients come from one's book; meaning that people who start by first reading your shook tend to be more educated, affluent and loyal. Combine this versatility with the powerful positioning and authority-building credibility of being an author and you can see why I think most business owners should be shook authors!

However, getting a shook done is only the first part of the equation. I'm sure you've probably heard (and maybe even experienced yourself) of a person spending months writing their book and a year later they still have unopened boxes of books in storage.

After the initial "high" of getting their books and giving them to friends and family, the reality of everything needed to effectively use it brings them down, and often they end up doing little with their book, so they sit in boxes unused.

Whereas big publishers have the wherewithal to invest heavily in book promotion and tours, the average business owner doesn't have the time, money or interest to do all the things traditional book authors must do after writing their book.

After working with local, Main Street business owners for over two decades, it's clear to me they have unique needs and opportunities when it comes to leveraging a book in their business. Much of what traditional book marketing is all about is NOT what you need, which is why I developed my shook publishing program—the Main Street Author Program. I have also written an entire shook on ways to use a *free book* marketing strategy effectively—*The Magic of Free Books*.

Shooks are formulaic and focused. We are not worried about critical acclaim, mass public acceptance, best-seller lists or a writing style that would make your high school teachers proud. Shooks are essentially sales letters put into book format and shook-centric marketing is all about attracting ideal readers for the shook and helping them along the path of becoming a customer. There are three primary ways for you to leverage your shook, including:

- Before-Shook Marketing
- With-Shook Marketing
- After-Shook Marketing

This shook-centric marketing trifecta is uniquely designed for local business owners and gives them exactly what they need to effectively promote, leverage and profit from their shook. Let me give you a quick overview of each pillar.

Before-Shook Marketing

The primary focus of Before-Shook Marketing is about getting your shook into the hands of the targeted reader and using effective media to promote the shook and getting as many qualified people to get it, ask for it or buy it. Instead of focusing your marketing messages on product and service benefits, they are focused on the shook and its promise of help.

"Have this problem? Get my book."

"Want to have this? Get my book."

"Need to learn more about this? Get my book."

The media options for Before-Shook Marketing are fairly long and consist of everything from articles to direct mail to strategic partners. Make sure you read my shook, *Marketing with Short Free Books* for 51 tactics you can use. Here are a few examples from the Before-Shook Marketing toolkit we created for Julie Steinbacher's shooks.

3D Shook Graphics

Strategic Partner Shook Display

FOR IMMEDIATE RELEASE
Contact: Amanda Anderson, (570) 322.2077

Two New Books Show Those Recently Diagnosed with Alzheimer's Disease and Their Caregivers How to Cope & Live

WILLIAMSPORT, April 1, 2019 – In 2019, millions of people will receive the shattering news of an Alzheimer's disease diagnosis. This new book, from a recognized local expert and elder-care attorney, shares critical information and guidance for people recently diagnosed with Alzheimer's disease.

In her two just-released books *You're Not Alone: Living with Alzheimer's Disease* and *You're Not Alone: Living as an Alzheimer's Caregiver*, author and local attorney Julieanne E. Steinbacher taps into her years of experience of helping people in the central Pennsylvania community to share current and must-have information to guide those recently diagnosed with Alzheimer's and their caregivers to cope, prepare and protect themselves. These short books are designed to be easy and quick to read and offers practical advice on exactly what one needs to do.

These timely and practical guides go beyond the general information available online and from healthcare organizations. These books show central-PA residents:

- Different options for care providers
- How to protect for themselves legally
- How to choose their decision makers
- How to plan for their pets
- How to deal with the stresses of caregiving
- Answers to the most common questions regarding Alzheimer's disease

"I've devoted my professional life to helping the elderly in our community and it pains me to see people in my community hit with the life-shattering news of an Alzheimer's disease diagnosis and not know what to do next. Nobody is prepared for this type of news and helping, and guiding patients is what I do each and every day," say Steinbacher. "There is a lot of confusing information out there and I wanted to author a simple and easy-to-read guide that offers critical 'next step' information, which is why I wrote this book and the companion book for caregivers."

Julieanne E. Steinbacher is the founding shareholder of Steinbacher, Goodall & Yurchak, an elder care and special needs law firm offering quality representation to clients throughout Pennsylvania. She is a nationally recognized authority on elder-care and has authored several related books. She has a "Superb" AVVO Rating for attorneys and was named a Super Lawyers Rising Star. Julieanne is a recipient of a 2015 Pennsylvania Bar Association (PBA) Special Achievement Award, which recognized her dedication and commitment to the PBA's Quality of Life /Balance Committee.

You're Not Alone: Living with Alzheimer's Disease and the companion book, *You're Not Alone: Living as an Alzheimer's Caregiver* are available at no cost from Julieanne's office. Call (570)322.2077, email info@paeldercounsel.com or visit either her Williamsport or State College offices.

Shook Announcement Media Release

IS ALZHEIMER'S DISEASE IMPACTING YOU OR YOUR FAMILY?

Two New Books by Local Elder Care Attorney, Julieanne Steinbacher, Shows Those Recently Diagnosed and Their Caregivers How to Cope

WILLIAMSPORT >> In 2019, it's estimated more than 5 million Americans will be affected by Alzheimer's Disease, which is why local elder law attorney, Julieanne Steinbacher has published two new short books for people who have been impacted by Alzheimer's Disease.

Each is designed to be read in about an hour and gives readers a helpful path of information and encouragement based on years of experience in helping others on the same journey.

You're Not Alone: Living with Alzheimer's Disease was written for the person who has been recently diagnosed with Alzheimer's and encourages and guides them to prepare for this chapter in life.

Each chapter in this easy-to-read book provides important information and resources to protect loved ones (including pets) and maintain independence for as long as possible.

The second book, *You're Not Alone: Living as an Alzheimer's Caregiver* is written for family members and loved ones who are caring for those with Alzheimer's Disease.

These individuals need to know what resources are available to help them as they help their loved one and this book offers an excellent collection of tips, ideas and resources available.

In describing why she published these two books, Julieanne shared the following comments.

"I've been a lifelong resident of this area and I've seen hundreds of individuals and families affected by Alzheimer's Disease. The news of diagnosis and the responsibility of care that goes along with it are profound and life-changing."

She continues, "It's my personal mission in life to help, encourage and guide both the diagnosed and his or her caregivers. I want them to truly know, they are not alone and my team and I are here to help when needed."

For a limited time, Julieanne is giving away copies of each book for free. There is no obligation and you can read them in the privacy and comfort of your home. Get this important information today!

4 WAYS TO GET YOUR FREE BOOK(S):

We are happy to send you free copies of these books and we will even mail them for free too! There's no obligation, we just want to be there for you when you need us.

There are four ways you can request your book(s):

1) Go to Julie's website at www.paeldercounsel.com/books
2) Call the office at (570) 322.2077
3) Fax the office at (570) 322.2119
4) Visit Julie's office at
413 Washington Blvd
Williamsport, PA 17701

Shook Advertorial

Shook Lead Generation Postcard

Shook Lead Generation Print Advertisements

With-Shook Marketing

With-Shook Marketing is all about specific assets that are sent or included with the shook when it's distributed. The primary focus of With-Shook Marketing is to make a big impact and get the person to read the shook and take the next step. Examples include unique packaging, personalized cover letters, special gifts and other marketing collateral.

WOW! Kit for Prospects

One of my favorite strategies I use for myself and my shook clients is the development of a Shook WOW! Kit. You may have heard them referred to as "shock and awe" packages.

WOW! Kit for Clients

Regardless, this is a strategically designed marketing kit, which is used to get attention and WOW the person receiving it. Our WOW! Kit includes a strategic set of customized collateral and full-color boxes that are sized exactly for shooks and the included marketing materials.

I use my WOW! Kit in two different ways:

1. I send them to shook client prospects and include copies of the shooks I want to send them. I also include a handwritten thank you card and a variety of marketing pieces.

2. I send them to individuals when they join my Main Street Author Program and include different shooks and a few valuable gifts, including a personalized "thank you" shook and JournalBook™ they can use for notetaking during our coaching calls.

Shook WOW! Kits are an effective way to building a fun and attention-grabbing kit around your shook and related marketing collateral.

After-Shook Marketing

After-Shook Marketing is all about the follow-up with shook readers and doing everything possible to help them along and convert them into paying customers. Specific online and offline strategies are used, including downloadable bonuses, email and mail follow-up.

The big takeaway for you is this—having a printed shook ready to be used is smart, fulfilling and full of profit potential.

The key word is **potential**.

Boxes of unused shooks in storage don't help your prospects and are only valuable when being read by your idea reader.

Working together, we can ensure you not only achieve the enviable status of "author" but also leverage the benefits of a shook-centric marketing system, working for you 24/7. To get you started

The Business Owner's Guide to Using a "Free Book"
Marketing Strategy to Attract New Customers

THE MAGIC OF
FREE BOOKS

PROVEN   EFFECTIVE   STRATEGIC   VALUABLE

MIKE CAPUZZI

thinking about all the different ways you can leverage your shook, make sure you get your copy of *The Magic of Free Books*. You can get it here:

MarketingWithFreeBooks.com

The irresistible offer of a *free book* has been used for over 120 years by savvy businesses to leverage the promise of a short, helpful book to identify ideal prospects and begin a mutually beneficial relationship.

If you are looking to build a profitable and sustainable marketing engine for your business that constantly churns out qualified prospects 24 hours a day, 7 days a week, 52 weeks a year 24/7/365, then *The Magic of Free Books* is a must-read!

Inside this treasure chest of smart ideas, I share my most effective book-marketing tactics on how to use a *free book* profitably to attract new customers (clients, patients, students, members, etc.).

It's a known fact that consumers who are book readers tend to be more educated, affluent and appreciative of helpful information when it comes to buying products and services, which is why creating a shook and giving it away is so smart. Put a few of these tactics to work for you and watch what happens!

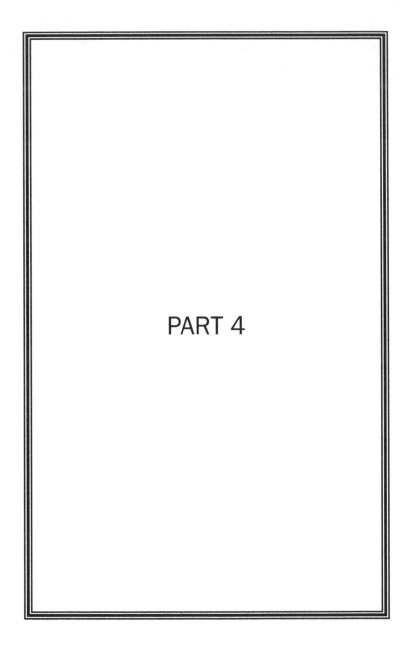

PART 4

THE PATH FORWARD

SHOOK IN ACTION

Title:	*Snore No More!*
Author:	Ricardo Guillen, DDS
Shook hook:	Discover an effective alternative to using a CPAP machine
Page count:	100
Active CTA:	Call his office to schedule an initial consultation
Passive CTA:	Get a free pulse oximeter

CHAPTER 9

HOW I HELP BUSINESS OWNERS BECOME AUTHORS

I hope by now you're convinced a short, helpful book to be used as the centerpiece of a *free book* marketing strategy is a must-have and valuable asset for you and your business.

I published my first book in 2007 and helped my first client publish his first book in 2008. For several subsequent years, I helped clients publish a variety of different short books. And in early 2019, I formalized my publishing service and created Bite Sized Books, which is specialized for two types of business owners:

1. The local Main Street business owner who has a place of business that people visit in order to buy their products and/or services (e.g., dentists, retailers, physicians, insurance agents, etc.).

2. The business owner who serves local Main Street business owners (e.g., software providers, service providers, consultants and coaches, etc.).

Bite Sized Books
Is Unique Because:

We are a "small-batch" publishing company that only serves local business owners or those business owners that serve local business owners, and we do so for these three reasons:

1. **We only publish short books that can be read in about an hour or two** (typically less than 15,000 words) and are written and designed to be a marketing and sales asset. Our shooks follow a classic "direct response marketing" formula.

2. **Our business owners/authors are not focused on trying to make money by selling their books**, but instead, will leverage the time-tested *free book* marketing strategy and give their book to as many qualified readers as possible.

3. **I am your primary point of contact, and you will only work directly with me**. I do not shlep you off to an assistant or inexperienced newbie. Instead, you are working with a successful and experienced fellow business owner, who has been helping clients improve their marketing since 1998. This gives you the peace of mind you deserve when working with a publishing partner.

Straight-Forward, Cost-Effective Options for Publishing Your Book

The reality is there are a bunch of places where you can make costly mistakes when publishing a book for your business. Considerable time should be given to the content, structure, goals and promotion of your shook, and this cannot be done in an hour or two, or even in a day. At least not in my opinion.

My Main Street Author Program offers you several straightforward, simple and cost-effective publishing options, and if you have read this far, I am sure one is ideal for you.

All of our options include everything you need to go from idea to printed book. And regardless of the option you choose, know that when you work with me, in whatever capacity, you benefit from my decades of experience, making sure you don't stall, trip or fumble.

When we work together, you will get the best of me working for you, and you get an all-inclusive and personalized opportunity to get your shook done right and done fast. We will have scheduled phone calls, and you will have direct access to me, as I guide you step-by-step. Before you know it, you will be a Main Street author and have a professionally published shook working for you and your business.

What You See Is What You Get

I believe in being honest, straightforward and transparent, which is why I put all the details and pricing for our Main Street Author Program right on our website.

BiteSizedBooks.com/program

Why Am I Laying This Out
So Clearly?

Because I see no reason to hide this information or wait until we talk to share all the details with you. I strongly believe in the power and value of having your own shook as quickly as possible. Therefore, I want to help you act swiftly by enabling you to make the best decision for you and your business.

Note that while our Main Street Author Program options are not inexpensive, they are far less than other publishers. And I have done my best to pack as much value into them as possible to ensure you get exactly what you need for a fair price.

So now that you know exactly who we are interested in helping as well as what we do and how much it all costs, I want to invite you to take...

CHAPTER 10

THE NEXT STEP

Congratulations! You are one step closer to writing your first (or next) book. I hope I have opened your eyes to a new opportunity and you are excited about the potential of working together and publishing your own short, helpful book!

Imagine what it will feel like to hold it and show it to your family with your name on the cover and your helpful words inside.

Think about the satisfaction you'll get when someone tells you, "I read your book and want to work with you."

Trust me, it's gratifying and makes the entire authoring and publishing effort worthwhile.

Having your own short, helpful book sets you apart from all the other people in your niche who are fighting for the same customers. Your own shook makes you special, and I can help you become an author with my proven "shook system" that has helped me and my clients publish shooks in all kinds of business categories.

Never Stop. Keep Moving Forward.

As I said earlier, I wrote this shook for two primary reasons: 1.) to help, inspire and motivate readers like you; 2.) to extend an invitation to see if working together to bring your shook to the world makes sense—for both of us.

If you like what you have read so far and feel like working directly with me to plan and publish your shook makes sense, let me ask you to consider these three questions and answer them in your mind.

1. *Would your ideal reader be in a better place if they read your future book?*

2. *Are you serious and committed to doing the work to get your book completed in 8–12 weeks?*

3. *Do you value working with an expert to guide you, bring out the best in you and prevent mistakes?*

If your answers are three yes's, then as I see it, you have three pathways in front of you at this very moment in time.

1. You can close this shook and do nothing with the information I shared. (If you have gotten this far, I surely hope this is not an option.)

2. You can start your shook—on your own—by leveraging the tips, tactics and strategies I have just given you.

3. You can prevent making any of the countless writing, publishing and marketing mistakes so many make, and schedule a **Shook Strategy Session** with me to discuss your nonfiction business-book ideas.

If you are serious about writing a good book—FAST—you have nothing to lose by choosing the third pathway.

This one call holds the key to unlocking the power and potential of your own short, helpful book.

There is no obligation, and scheduling it is super easy.

I understand your goals are uniquely yours, which is why you and I need to talk—if you are serious about authoring a customer-attraction book.

This call is all about helping you decide if working together to get your shook done is a good fit for both of us.

Maybe we are meant to work together. Maybe not.

But we will not know unless you and I have this first, critical conversation.

Note: It's NOT a Sales Call

It's a two-way interview to make sure we agree this is a good match.

I'll ask you some questions, and you can ask me some questions (in fact, as many questions as you want).

And then, we can go from there.

This is typically a 20- to 30-minute call, however, we will stay on until you're satisfied you are ready to work with me or you simply want to move on.

That's it. There is no obligation on your part.

Every author I have introduced to you in this shook all started with this same exact call. (See what they have to say about working with me by visiting **BiteSizedBooks.com/authors**.)

I am a firm believer you are uniquely qualified to be working with certain people—not everybody but people who "get" you and what you and your business stand for.

I feel the same about my business, and in order for us to see if we are a good fit, I have found these calls to be the ideal litmus test. It will give us a chance to "meet" and see if working together makes sense.

TODAY Is the Day. NOW Is the Time.

Will you step up to the challenge and create the short, helpful book your ideal reader needs and is looking for?

Your future customers are waiting, watching, and wanting you to.

Authoring and sharing your own shook is what you have been waiting for.

This is your call-to-action, and in my opinion, responsibility.

I challenge you to answer it.

You are ready.

Schedule your **Shook Strategy Session** with me right now. There's absolutely no fee, no obligation, no risk, and nothing to lose.

How to Schedule Our Call

Here's what to do:

1. Visit **BiteSizedBooks.com/program**.

2. Review my Main Street Author Program options and pricing to see which program is right for you and your business.

3. Click the Shook Strategy Session button and follow the prompts to schedule a call with me.

I look forward to hearing from you, and more importantly, working together to turn you into a Main Street author and helping you create one of the most powerful and effective marketing assets you can create for your business—your very own shook.

Thank you!

Mike

ABOUT MIKE CAPUZZI

Mike is a publisher, an Amazon #1 best-selling author, and coach for business owners looking to uniquely position themselves, differentiate their business and attract new customers easily by authoring and publishing a short, helpful book.

Throughout his two+ decades as a marketing strategist, Mike's innovative use of *high impact marketing* has consistently surpassed the expectations and outcomes of traditional marketing concepts and business strategies for his clients.

His expertise has led him to be a guest speaker on the stages of some of the world's most foremost experts on marketing, including Dan Kennedy and Bill Glazer. To date, Mike has helped thousands of business owners around the world create more effective and profitable marketing.

Mike is the inventor of the wildly successful library of hand-drawn, direct-response graphics known as CopyDoodles®. CopyDoodles are hand-drawn graphic files that enable anybody to literally drag and drop attention-grabbing enhancements to their offline and online marketing materials. Tens of thousands of business owners, marketers and copywriters have benefited from the use of CopyDoodles (check out **CopyDoodles.com**).

In 2019, Mike launched Bite Sized Books, a new publishing venture founded on his proven formula for creating short, helpful books (known as shooks) for business owners. Shooks are ideal for business owners who are looking to increase their level of authority, while also providing helpful information in bite sized books.

Mike is also the host of The Main Street Author Podcast where he interviews business owners and book experts on real-world, proven ways to leverage a book to position yourself and promote your business. Check it out at **MikeCapuzzi.com**, and if you think you would make a great guest (one that has written and published at least one printed book), visit **MikeCapuzzi.com/guest** to introduce yourself.

To learn more about Mike's opportunities, visit **MikeCapuzzi.com**, and if you're looking for a content-rich, unique speaker for your in-person or virtual event or podcast, contact Mike for his speaker kit.

THE MAIN STREET AUTHOR PODCAST

The Main Street Author Podcast is an interview-style podcast with host, Mike Capuzzi, and local Main Street business owners who have successfully authored, published and leveraged a book in their business to differentiate themselves and attract more ideal customers, clients, patients or students.

Each episode is focused on book strategies that work for traditional local business owners. Even though you may have never heard of some of Mike's guests, you're sure to get several ideas and nuggets of wisdom that are proven to work in the real world of face-to-face business.

Listen at MikeCapuzzi.com and if you think you would make a suitable guest on the Main Street Author Podcast, visit MikeCapuzzi.com/guest and connect with Mike.

THE SHOOK SUCCESS SERIES

Over the past several years, I have authored a number of shooks to show business owners around the world how to author, self-publish and use these powerful marketing assets in their business. Besides sharing a wealth of powerful ideas, tips and knowledge, each of these shooks is a prime example of how to craft and use a short, helpful book.

The Magic of Short Books goes into detail on how to author your own shook, including all the components you need to include.

The Magic of Free Books shares 51 marketing tactics to leverage and make money with your shook.

Main Street Author goes into how local business owners use shooks to promote themselves and their business.

The 100-Page Book is my Amazon #1 Best Seller that describes an even shorter shook to consider.

Get them at **MikeCapuzzi.com/author**.

A SMALL REQUEST

Thank you for reading *The Magic of Short Books*! I am positive if you follow what I've written, you will be on your way to being a published author!

When you do, please send me a copy of your shook so I can show it off! I have a small, quick favor to ask. Would you mind taking a minute or two and leaving an honest review for this shook on Amazon? Reviews are the BEST way to help others purchase this shook, and I check all my reviews looking for helpful feedback. Visit:

MikeCapuzzi.com/tmsb

If you have any questions or if you would just like to tell me what you think about *The Magic of Short Books*, shoot an email to info@mikecapuzzi.com. I'd love to hear from you!

DON'T FORGET THIS!

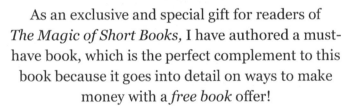

As an exclusive and special gift for readers of *The Magic of Short Books,* I have authored a must-have book, which is the perfect complement to this book because it goes into detail on ways to make money with a *free book* offer!

The Magic of Free Books is an advanced book that I wrote to show business owners 51 specific and proven tactics to turn a *free book* into new customers. There is **NO OTHER BOOK** like it and you can **ONLY GET IT HERE...**

SPECIAL READER BONUS

www.MarketingWithFreeBooks.com

Made in the USA
Las Vegas, NV
14 January 2022

41392401R00075